The Dumping Ground

The Dumping Ground

Copyright © 2015 –Latasha Matthews

Scripture quotations are taken from the King James Version Bible ©1979, 1980, 1982 by Thomas Nelson, Inc. Publishers. All rights reserved.

Scripture quotations are taken from the New Living Translation Bible ©1979, 1980, 1982 by Thomas Nelson, Inc. Publishers. All rights reserved.

Printed in the United States of America

First eBook edition: 2015
First print book edition: 2015

ISBN-10: 0692584439

ISBN-13: 978-0692584439

Through Words Publishing, LLC
Severn, MD 21144

THROUGH WORDS
PUBLISHING, LLC

Dedication

I would like to dedicate this book to my good friend Tonya Taylor (since 2012) who encouraged me to take the limits off and take hold of everything God has for me.

I would also like to dedicate this book to those people who have the courage to set boundaries despite the possible consequences that come with you taking care of yourself.

Acknowledgements

I would first like to thank God for giving me the inspiration and placing the wonderful gift of compassion and sharing on the inside of me.

I would also like to thank my dad, mom and sister for listening to my vision of the book and many other ideas to come. Your belief in me is amazing.

I would like to give some special thanks to Antonina Geer, my longtime friend for giving me the courage. You provided me with a good example of an authentic author.

Tanisha Sapp, my writing coach and friend, you have been my strong sounding board on everything and I thank you very much.

A special thank you to my Pastor Vincent Campbell who barely knows me but found it beneficial to read, pray and provide support for me in so many ways.

I would also like to thank Gwendolyn Young for helping me develop the structure and system to write this book and motivating me to do it.

Thank you Talisa Beasley for allowing me to bounce ideas off of you for the next 5 book titles and the countless other friends and colleagues that have offered to share my information, read chapters, wear merchandise and help market the book.

Many thanks to my amazing assistant who listens to me ramble on and created any and everything I ask him to create. You are a creative genius Jarrod Walker and I thank you.

I cannot forget my clients who allow me to be very transparent and share pieces of myself and the book throughout our time together.

Lastly, I would also like to thank the readers known and unknown who will purchase and share "The Dumping Ground" movement with others.

Thank you Terry Freeman, LPC owner of Freeman Counseling & Consulting, LLC, one of my amazing therapist, for providing me the support and education regarding the importance of setting boundaries.

Foreword

If you are anything like me, in life you've really messed some things up. However, if it had not been for the grace of God, things would have been much worse. I can recall that in certain areas of my life, at the helm of some of those mess ups is when "no" or "not now" should have been my answer. Experiences where had I truly consulted God or waited for His timing as well as direction in relationships, business endeavors, financial matters, and career moves, the outcomes would have been different. What it really boils down to is I didn't have Godly boundaries established. Therefore, without having boundaries I had no standards in which to filter every choice and decision made.

Contrary to what some may believe Godly boundaries are not restrictions or regulations that keep us from enjoying life. They are not some set of rules that God made up and uses to punish us. In fact, they are quite the opposite. God gives us boundaries because He loves us and wants to protect us from the parts of ourselves where we struggle to exhibit self-control. In fact, He loves us so much that He gives us a choice to live within His boundaries or live outside of them. However, always gently speaking to us and guiding us in the right direction, but leaving it up to us to choose.

What I love most about Godly boundaries is that they are more about your heart of surrender and your willingness to come to the end of yourself so that you can become who God wants you to be and experience Him in the full. They are essential to the abundant life God desires for all of us as we live out His plan.

I was reminded of this truth as I read through Latasha Matthews book "The Dumping Ground". This book is a tool that will encourage and inspire you to evaluate every area of your life and yield you to God. It will assist you to establish boundaries where there are none, and re-establish boundaries where you may have forgotten.

In this book Latasha pours out of her heart what she's learned and continues to learn about establishing boundaries in her own life. Throughout the years I've seen her live, fight, weep, and triumph through a myriad of experiences. Some of which at the time though it may not have been evident then, were clearly teaching lessons of creating boundaries and implementing them in every area of her life. Not only for her benefit, but so that she through her transparency and honesty can teach from an authentic place through "The Dumping Ground" series of books.

I've had the privilege of knowing Latasha and being in close friendship with her for fifteen years. She is an amazingly loving teacher, counselor, and friend. I am grateful to have her in my life as a sister-friend for so many years and love her dearly. Many times I've been on the receiving end of her wisdom as I journeyed through different experiences of my life. I am blessed to be able to also learn from being there during some of Latasha's life moments as she lived and walked out Godly boundaries in different phases of her life. Now, because of "The Dumping Ground" the world gets to experience what I've been honored to have in my life for so long.

This book will be a blessing to you and as you implement what you learn from it. It can be the foundation of a turning point in your life. As you read through this book have an open heart of surrender knowing that boundaries established in God's will and standards are a gift of love. They are a gift of freedom that when you choose to receive it and live life by it, you will clear the way for more abundance that God has for you.

May your life be full of love, joy, and peace as you live within God's boundaries!

Antonina D. Geer, MBA

Table of Contents

Preface

Hi my name is Latasha Matthews and I am a Licensed Professional Counselor and Life Coach in Lawrenceville, Georgia. I have learned that God teaches me by teaching others; however, before you can teach others honesty is required regarding the areas you just totally botched up. For a long time I had difficulty being transparent and vulnerable in sharing my mess-ups and shortcomings, but who am I really hiding from? So, I began the journey of self-discovery, honesty and vulnerability, which enabled me to utilize my truth to facilitate the growth and healing of others. My clients and I have very similar stories and I was unable to deny the work that was required of me as I helped them along the way.

The "Dumping Ground" was birthed out of my inability to set the boundaries that God requires. This topic is very close to my heart because it has cost me a tremendous amount of pain and consequences that have significantly shaped the course of my life. Financial losses, sickness, relationship challenges, poor decisions and a host of other consequences will come if you are unable to set effective boundaries. I found it necessary to share out of obedience to God but also because so many people that I have encountered and have come in contact with, experience or have experienced the same challenges with boundary setting. The vast majority of what I write about I have experienced firsthand in some aspect. So I pray that this book provides you practical tools and a clear understanding of why it is so imperative to set life – saving boundaries.

So why the title the Dumping Ground?

Well, I'm a visual person and I learn best by what I see. So when I began to think about all of the challenges I have experienced and the people I have encountered with similar challenges, I had a vision. The visual image that came to mind was a dump truck filled with garbage dumping trash onto a person who was standing behind the truck. That visual represented the feeling and experiences I felt before I realized that I had the power, ability and the right to take care Tasha first. Awareness was the first critical step for me. Awareness allowed me to seek guidance from God on his desires for me. God began to speak to me about how he wanted me to protect myself and how he had all these wonderful gifts to give me but without limits and self-restraint I continued to miss these gifts.

In Galatians 5:22-23, it highlights some of God's precious gifts. He said he wanted to give me peace; but without setting boundaries my peace was always situational and stolen by someone, something or myself. He said he wants to show me love; but without setting boundaries I gave that love away to those undeserving and to those who did not have my best interests at heart. He wants to give me wisdom and understanding; but without boundaries I leaned on my own understanding and the understanding of others. He wants to give me joy but without boundaries my joy was based on things that wavered. He wants to teach me longsuffering; but without boundaries I crumbled and cracked. He wants to teach me how to handle the gift of kindness but when pushed beyond my limits my kindness turns into anger. He wants to give me gentleness because he has been gentle with me, but without boundaries in place I am rough and harsh. Lastly, he desires to teach me self-control; because without it I go to places and do things that are outside of his will for my life and that always leads to destruction. God offered me these gifts and many others; however, I was unable to access them due to inability set boundaries.

So what are boundaries?

Webster's dictionary defines boundaries as unofficial rules of what should be done and limits that define acceptable behavior. Boundaries are designed for protection. They were created to aid in helping you maintain accountability for the things you value. Boundaries also help you identify and clarify what are acceptable and unacceptable behaviors not only from others but also from yourself. At times we as people don't always treat ourselves well. We often self-destruct, self-sabotage, and internally victimize ourselves. Just as doors, fences, and windows protect our property, boundaries should be in place to protect our spirit, our mind, and our bodies.

So one might ask, where do boundaries come from and who needs boundaries anyway? I'm sure we all have several answers that come to mind. Here is my answer and I am sticking to it, first thing first, boundaries must be taught. In reality, some of us are at a deficit in this area. There are a vast majority of people who come from families that have displayed unhealthy boundaries; physically, financially, sexually, emotionally, and most importantly spiritually. For individuals who came from stable families that had healthy boundaries in place that taught you how to have realistic limits and guidelines that govern your life, this book will help you continue to maintain those boundaries. I am of the belief that God created those boundaries through his Son Jesus Christ and the Holy Spirit. If we allow, the Holy Spirit enforces and provides guidance in maintaining those boundaries.

For those who do not have a relationship with Christ, I offer you that opportunity to accept Him right here while you are reading these words. Romans 10:9, states, "If you confess with your mouth and believe in your heart that God raised Him from the dead you will be saved. This is the key to salvation, just simply believing,

For anyone who would like to learn practical steps to set limits for yourself this book is for you. So I thank you for taking this journey with me to learn powerful ways to set life-changing boundaries that will save your life. I hope that this book provides healing as you read.

Introduction

Have you ever wondered why some people are able to delegate tasks and get things done and others are not? Have you ever wondered why some people are often rushing from one place to the next while others have lots of time to relax and enjoy life? Have you ever thought about how it would feel to take care of yourself before thinking of others? What would it feel like to get all your needs met? What about finances; why do some people have more than enough and others do not? Well to be very honest I have thought about these things and I'm sure that others ponder these questions and thoughts as well. These questions and many others ignited my passion and desire to write *The Dumping Ground.* We all have access to answer all these questions; however, we tend to lose focus on getting our needs met at times. There's a saying, that life is what you make it; however, what I found in life is not the case. You must be intentional about doing some things in life to have fulfillment.

One area I found particularly challenging and even rippling at times is boundary setting. When you are not equipped to understand the importance of setting boundaries in your life you become the dumping ground for your spouse, your kids, your friends, your boss, your finances, your health and many other areas in life.

This book is designed to help you identify your worth and give you an understanding of the importance of boundary setting. It will also give you the skills needed to set life changing boundaries.

Happy boundary setting!!!!

Chapter 1

Skirting the Issue

Skirting the issue deals with how we communicate authentically. The proper term for skirting the issue is avoidance. Webster's dictionary defines avoidance as keeping away from, clear or prevent from happening. We avoid things for reasons such as: fear, rejection or skill deficits. Avoidance can cause severe consequences to include: dishonesty, anxiety, stress, unhealthy relationships, unbalanced schedule, health problems, spiritual conflicts and depression.

Let's look at how skirting the issue impacted Maria

Maria was a successful businesswoman who worked hard to climb the corporate ladder. She had a great relationship with her boss who challenged her to be the best person she could be. Maria truly valued her supervisor's opinion and the opinion of all the executive leadership team, as she never had anyone to validate her. She had a horrible childhood; which included a horrible relationship with her parents. She felt like her relationships with her co-workers and superiors were really satisfying. Maria stated that she would do anything to make sure these relationships remain intact. After all, her work relationships were the closest resemblance to her family. Maria was married with two small children and found herself juggling to meet the demands of her family and her job. Maria did not feel the same way about her family nor did she receive the validation from her husband or children. All Maria thought about was the very high demands and expectations that her boss placed on her. Her husband began to notice that Maria was coming home later and later. She started missing important aspects at home, such as bible study, the kids sporting events and not to mention the household chores that were neglected. Her husband began talking to her about this but she became angry and refused to listen. The arguments became more regular and that brought distance between her and her husband. Maria started to resent the fact that she had to care for her children and her husband. Eventually, she began to question her marriage vows that she made to God and her husband. It wasn't until Maria was terminated from her job, due to budget cuts that she realized that she had totally skirted the true issues while neglecting her family and her relationship with God.

How many times have we skirted the issue ourselves and it has cost us greatly. At a glance you would think Maria was overly concerned about the success of her job but at the core Maria was unable to set boundaries because she had a deep-rooted need for approval.

I know all too well how it feels to need and desire the approval from others. As I reflected on all those situations, I was unaware that God had already approved me. There was a time that I didn't know that His approval was truly all I needed. As areas of my life continued to crumble I continued to seek approval by attempting to climb the corporate ladder. I thought that by seeking additional certifications and working later hours that my supervisor would like me and treat me well. My supervisor asked me to do things that that I knew were not pleasing to me or God, but I did those things to gain favor and validation from her. I also thought that seeking approval from co-workers would make me feel good about myself. Have you ever hung out with the wrong crowd, knowing you didn't have anything in common with them just to get their approval and validation that you were good enough? Well I did and I became emptier and emptier only to find myself lost. When I was laid off by my supervisor I truly had time to reflect. It wasn't the people at work who had the problem, it was me. The supervisor I thought was my friend and mentor laid me off without notice because it was never about me. I finally figured out that you cannot please man. I also realized that a lot of the actions I took to gain my supervisor's approval were unethical and hurtful towards others.

Joyce Meyer talks about approval addiction in her book entitled, *Approval Fix.* She believes that there is a cure for the approval addiction which is the Word of God. Joyce explained that the knowledge of who we are in Christ is the cure. She goes on to explain the righteousness we have through Christ gives us the authority to set boundaries. God's love for us must be enough for us to begin to remove the desire to seek approval from the world. God talks about his love for us in Ephesians 1:4 (NLT): "Even before he made the world, God loved us and chose us in Christ to be holy and without fault in his eyes." This scripture represents love from the One who validates us and makes us whole.

The Dump:

1. Identify the areas that you fear and avoid. Write down the worst thing that could happen if that fear is realized. Write down ways that you can handle that fear if it came to pass.

2. Imagine and write down how you might feel if these areas didn't exist in your life.

3. Write down the consequences that you have faced for avoiding situations or area of your life.

4. Have you ever felt like Maria? If so, how did you handle it? What ways can you address this boundary issue?

5. What does validation mean to you? Have you ever sought approval from others? How did it impact your life?

   Main Point: Seeking approval from the world will always end in destruction.

Pledge: I pledge to identify the core issues and work towards resolving them.

Reflection: There is no need to skirt the issues we face in life. Setting healthy emotional boundaries for yourself and identifying healthy ways to get your needs met is a crucial way to establish a boundary.

Chapter 2

Diamonds & Pearls
Just Won't Do

If you are not familiar with diamonds you would have to look very close to determine its authenticity. When determining legitimacy perhaps you would look at clarity or the cut of the diamond. Some would look at the size to make a determination on its trueness. There are a number of tests that you can conduct to tell the difference between a genuine diamond and a fake one. The genuineness of a diamond is important because it measures its true value.

In my practice I speak with people daily that struggle with being true and authentic. At times it is extremely difficult to be transparent and real. I admit that I have also struggled with this because it is very easy to represent different faces. It is much easier to mask our true selves in fear of not being accepted. What I've come to realize is that you and I are really not any different from the diamond. Our value is measured internally and not externally. To understand your purpose and value, you must seek clarity from the One who created you and begin the process of being true to yourself. So my question to you is will you represent who God created you to be or be a counterfeit?

Tavia had everything in life but a man. She had her eye on a successful entrepreneur who had everything going for him. However, he paid Tavia little or no attention, which made Tavia even more determined to get him. She positioned herself in the same circles to meet this man and when given the opportunity to meet Marvin for a business opportunity she completely misrepresented herself to gain his loyalty. She beefed up her resume and learned the common jargon in his business unit to present herself as knowledgeable. He found her quite sharp and intelligent and he was very attracted to those characteristics. They eventually became business partners and later lovers. She continued to lie about her career, her work experience and her character to keep this man. When the lies were finally exposed he left her and made her name a disgrace among other colleagues. Tavia did not have an understanding of her worth. All of her value was wrapped up in gaining favor from Marvin but later she found out that no matter how she represented herself to Marvin she would never be valuable in his eyes.

Knowing and accepting your self-worth will directly impact how you see yourself. This will determine what boundaries you will set to be with a man or to prove yourself to anyone. Tavia had no limits and she did just about anything to make herself appear to be that glistening diamond for Marvin. Without internal love for yourself you will seek approval from others and you will begin to look outside of yourself to gain favor from others. God has given all of us the necessary ingredients within; therefore, He validates and covers us. In addition, He has given us the ability to develop those attributes and gifts that He has placed on the inside of us for His purpose. If you seek God's purpose for your life, it will help you set the appropriate guidelines and boundaries. Your inability to set a boundary based on your true self will cost you tremendously.

I am sure we can all relate to some aspect of Tavia's story at some point in life. I can personally relate to Tavia. Several years ago I dated a gentleman who had an idealistic approach regarding the type of women he wanted to date from a spiritual perspective. He was very religious and he wanted someone who could match his intellect when it came to God. Well of course I did not see this as a problem at first. Nonetheless, I found myself trying to convince this man that I was a bible scholar knowing that I was not. In my mind, I was on "his level" but it was never enough. He became very judgmental and to my surprise began to question my faith. At this point it started to make me feel inferior. A few things I did not consider was that God cares very little about religious antics, how much you know or how versed you are in quoting scriptures. God cares about your heart for Him and His people. He cares about your spirit and your soul.

Now let's be clear, this story is not a male bashing session, it is only shared to point out my inability to consult the God who created me and defined my value and worth. In fact David speaks about how important we are to God, in Psalms 139-13-16. He says, "For you formed my inward parts; you knitted me together in my mother's womb. I praise you, for I am fearfully and wonderfully made. Wonderful are your works; my soul knows it very well. My frame was not hidden from you, when I was being made in secret, intricately woven in the depths of the earth. Your eyes saw my unformed substance; in your book were written, every one of them, the days that were formed for me, when as yet there was none of them." This scripture alone shows God's ability to define our value.

The Dump:

1. Are you being true to your unique, authentic self? Give examples.

2. Identify your unique attributes and explain how they are valuable.

3. If you are unable to think of unique attributes, write down the attributes you wish or desire to have.

4. How does God view you?

Main Point: God defines your value and wealth.

Pledge: I pledge to not allow people, places or things to define my worth.

Reflection: God took His time creating someone special. You are valuable in His eyes. You are the apple of His eye.

Chapter 3

A Dance with Money

I remember a song that had a hook that said, "I work hard for the money"; for most people this is not a cliché it's a fact. Most of us would agree that money does not always come easy. With education, entrepreneurship, and the changing economy, resources are very important to us. Unfortunately, we live in a litigious society where others find ways to take advantage of your resources. Boundaries as it relates to finances are crucial aspects of life. You will find yourself always robbing Peter to pay Paul if you are unable to set guidelines for your money.

Check out David's story:

David loved to give. He enjoyed the fact that he had a great job and he lived life to the fullest. However, David had a problem with money. On a weekly basis he gave his mother who also had a good job, money for miscellaneous items. His mother would call him and give him a sob story about something she needed. David would give her the money because he had a good heart and that was the right thing to do. In addition, his co-workers would ask him to borrow money and he would graciously give and justify it by saying this is what a person does from the heart. David would never ask for the money back or even question his co-workers or his mom about money. David bought and gave lavish gifts and never really considered using wisdom. He never really considered the future, he lived for today. David found himself in a world of debt but because he continued to make money he never considered this a problem. David thought that because he used coupons and discounts at times that he had the right to shop; therefore, he justified his shopping. He eventually had to file bankruptcy and he lost everything.

David's' story might seem extreme but I am sure there are elements or pieces of his story that you can relate to. I know I can relate because I experienced some similar challenges that forced me to file bankruptcy as well. For many years I thought that it was ok to take lavish trips because I worked hard for them. With no husband or kids, I thought to myself this is the life of a single independent woman. I wasn't taught the importance of saving and managing my finances and to be honest it wasn't always modeled for me consistently in my home. Although, adulthood gave me the opportunity to change those behaviors, I had no boundaries or ideas on budgeting. I continued to spend and buy any and every thing I wanted. It made me feel good to spend money until one year I was laid off from my job with no money saved to survive. I used all my credit cards and student loans to live off of for quite some time. Unfortunately, when I started working my salary did not support all the bills I had incurred. I decided to file bankruptcy which affected me emotionally and financially as I started to grow my business. Not setting boundaries in your finances is stressful and will cause you to live in bondage. It also limits your ability to truly be able to give genuinely. You then begin to worry about things you cannot pay and live in fear as it pertains to your finances.

I thought spending money and having nice things validated a part of me but after the dust settled it has always caused major destruction in my life. I'm sure some of you reading this right now, are thinking that this is not my issue; however, I would suggest that you continue reading further.

The focus of this chapter is really to discuss entitlement and impulse control as it pertains to your finances. Despite your bills being paid and the amount of money in the bank, do you have the ability to control your spending? Does spending and purchasing validate or complete you? Do the clothes and jewelry you wear make you feel good? Can you do without those things? Are you spending and paying off a credit card each month because you have the money to do so? Do you feel entitled to have things because you work hard?

The bible addresses what God's desire is for our finances and His desire for us to prosper. In John 10:10, it states, "The thief cometh not, but for to steal and kill and to destroy: I am come that they might have life, and that they might have it more abundantly." You cannot have abundance in anything if you are unable to set limits. You will always have lack or want things. This is ultimately a distraction and a trick of the enemy because God promises to supply every last one of our needs. I had a parent who was a spender and the other was a saver. They were unable to get on one accord as it pertained to their finances.

Ultimately, this caused a major distraction to the family unit which impacted their ability to connect with one another and set sound examples for their children.

Being a good steward over the resources that God has given us is an important aspect in boundary setting. If you do not have a good relationship with money this will be an area that will filter over into others areas of your life.

The Dump

1. Identify and ask why you feel the need to help others.

2. Define your relationship with money. Do you have a healthy relationship with money? What would you change?

3. Name 3 ways can you begin to set appropriate boundaries with your money.

4. Do you feel entitled to spend?

Main Point: You must budget your money and plan to give.

Pledge: I pledge to be a good steward over my resources.

Reflection: Setting healthy limits around money will minimize stress, anxiety and relationship issues.

Chapter 4

Can't Hear You:
Are You Using Your Voice Effectively

God has given all of us many gifts but in my opinion one of the most amazing gifts is our voice. There is power in words. What we say can be used to uplift, encourage and motivate. Consequently, we can also use words to teardown, condemn and destroy. On the other hand, what we do not say can have a very similar effect on our life as well.

I have worked with countless numbers of clients that have struggled to access their voice within. I have found that if you use effective communication skills and understanding that there is power in your voice. You will not have effective boundaries if you are unable to use your voice.

In my research, I have found that there are several communication styles. One style is the passive communicator, who cringes at the thought of speaking up to get their needs met. This type of communicator normally has a difficult time being honest about their feelings. They will complain a lot about how people might take advantage of them because they are unable to express how they are feeling. Next, we have the aggressive communicator, who tends to use their voice ineffectively to control others. This communicator is forceful and asserts power to get their way. Lastly, is the assertive communicator, they are skilled in communicating effectively. They utilize their ability to communicate to get their needs meet. This type of communicator values their needs and respects the needs of others. They advocate for themselves and set boundaries to get what they need.

So guess which types of communicators primarily have boundary issues? For our conversation we will focus on the passive and aggressive communicators. These types of communicators often have a terrible time setting boundaries. Meet Michelle:

Michelle had her weekend planned out, she wanted to relax, watch TV and veg out on the couch. Why not, it was Saturday and she worked hard all week. However, what typically happens on Saturday is that her sister would call her in a crisis and ask her to keep the kids. So this time Michelle had her plan in place. She decided that she would not answer the phone and she would turn off the ringer to keep her from feeling guilty about not answering. She was certain that taking these steps would allow her to continue to enjoy her day.

Unfortunately, her enjoyment came to an abrupt end when she heard a knock at the door. It was her sister who stated that she had an emergency and that she had been calling her for hours. Her sister scolded her for not answering and begged her to keep the children. Before Michelle could answer the kids came in the house and made themselves at home. Shortly after that her sister ran out of the house stating that she would be back in a few hours. Well, Michelle rationalized this in her mind by stating it's not that bad, she said she would be back in a few hours. Michelle also justified it by stating that she is happy that she gets to spend time with her nieces. She knew she had committed to attend several events later on so she decided to make the best of it by relaxing and spending some time entertaining the kids. After she settled in with the kids she received a text message from a friend stating that he was stranded at the airport and wanted her to pick him up. Michelle struggled with this internally but never told her friend that she was busy and had lots of things going on. So she gathered up the kids and headed to the airport. This friend rarely calls but when he does call it is definitely when he needs something. Michelle was irritated but she headed to the airport. After she arrived at the airport , she call her friend several times only to find out that his flight would not arrive for another 2 hours. The flight had been delayed but he didn't bother calling her to let her know. Michelle felt bad leaving so she stayed and waited for her friend. While waiting on her friend to arrive Michelle pondered about how horrible her day was going. The kids were whining and arguing because they were hungry and bored. She also realized she had missed her massage appointment and she would incur a $30.00 cancellation fee. Michelle also realized that her sister had not called so she began to worry whether she would be on time for a dinner date with a girlfriend. So, Michelle got on the phone and began to attempt to reorganize her day, which was totally thrown off because of her sister. What do you think?

How many of us have been Michelle? I know I have had several weekends like Michelle. There is one word that comes to mind that she and many of us fail to use and it is a complete sentence; No. Using the word no is the best way to set a boundary. Unfortunately, for many of us it's much easier to go along with someone else's wishes instead of taking a stand to be assertive and firm. In my own life I juggle many hats and over committing use to be like drinking water for me. It happened often.

I remember a time during my weekend graduate program I would commit to playing in the line-up for my tennis team. I was always on pins and needles because tennis is not a timed sport. If it was time for my line to play and I wasn't there my team would have to forfeit that line of tennis. Not to mention, if I left too early from class, I would lose a letter grade. The excuse I made was I should be able to go to school and play tennis; however, once I committed to school, tennis had to come second. Setting boundaries with yourself is the first step in effective boundary setting because if you are unable to set boundaries with yourself you will never set boundaries with others.

Here are some questions to ponder if you are caught in a dilemma like Michelle.

The Dump:

1. Are my needs being met while helping others?

I know to some of you this question might sound selfish but it is ok to take care of yourself first. You should consider the reasons why you choose to put the needs of others before yours.

2. Are you proficient at saying no? If not, state the reasons why?

Practice makes perfect- Practice makes the perfect use of the word NO. With practice you do become more comfortable with using your voice. You have to weigh out the pros and cons and think about how you feel when your needs are not met.

3. Do I have the time to do whatever someone is asking of me?

You don't have to commit right away. You can get back to the person and truly determine if you have the time and interest. Don't commit unless it is something you want to do. Your needs come first, so slow down.

4. Does doing for others cause negative consequences?

5. Do I have the resources?

6. How is saying yes beneficial in this situation?

Main Point: You are just as important as others.

Pledge: I pledge to use assertive communication to get my need met.

Reflection: Saying no does not make you a bad person it actually makes you a healthy person with limits.

Chapter 5

Is it Worth My Time

Time as defined in the Webster dictionary is the measure or measurable period; in which, an action, process or condition, exists or continues. It is also defined as a continued process of existence and events in the past, present and future. I know what you are thinking; why am I giving you the definition of time? I am setting the stage on the importance of the word. Time is precious and in my opinion one of the biggest areas that is taken for granted. The assumption is that we will always have time. Often times we struggle with managing time appropriately. Time and boundary setting in my opinion has a direct or positive relationship. If you have a poor relationship or value of time you will often have issues in setting boundaries around your time.

Check out Renee's story:

Renee lived by her schedule. In her mind she had everything organized and planned out. She went from one meeting to the next. She called herself a scheduling machine, a super multi-tasker and get it done girl. Often time's Renee felt stretched and pulled in many directions because she thought there were 48 hours in one day instead of 24. Renee often procrastinated and felt unequipped to meet deadlines because she had so much on her plate. She did not have anything in her life that wasn't scheduled. Renee's schedule was always jammed packed. She found herself experiencing high levels of anxiety for things she didn't necessarily want to do. Her mood and emotions began to overwhelm her and she found herself missing critical appointments and people started to view her as flaky, irresponsible and unreliable. This caused even more anxiety and she began to ask herself; how did I get here? She thought she did a great job with managing her time but later realized she was over-extending herself doing a lot of things that are not worth her time.

So I ask, how many of us live by schedules that are piled up with things we really don't have to do nor want to do? I was just like Renee and it wasn't until I realized my life was precious and valuable that I began to set boundaries for myself. I started to experience life, instead of scheduling things that I identified as important for my life. I began to look at what I needed to do versus what I wanted to do. Setting boundaries with time helps promote balance, flexibility and a meaningful life.

The Dump

1. Identify 5 time busters that keep you from living the life you desire. Replace them with 5 productive activities you could be doing that will get you closer to your goal, purpose or vision.

2. If you have to place a dollar value on your current value of time, what dollar amount would you give it? What dollar value would you like to give it?

3. Now that you have identified the time busters here are a few questions to ask yourself.

4. Do you want to do this?

5. Can someone else do this?

6. Do I have the time?

7. How are these time busters impacting me emotionally, physically or spiritually?

Main Point: You must manage your time or it will manage you.

Pledge: I pledge to utilize my time to do things that enhance my purpose.

Reflection: God has given me enough time and I have the ability to manage it.

Chapter 6

Are You Willing to
Pay the Price

There is price to pay for not developing the necessary skills to set healthy boundaries. The price varies of course based on the situation and circumstances of the person but there are always emotional, spiritual and financial consequences that come from not setting appropriate boundaries. Boundaries are necessary for protection and serve as a reminder to us that we have limits and we have rights. Unfortunately, the expectation that others will respect or honor your boundaries is an irrational thought. Why would a person respect your boundaries if you are not willing to do the same?

Check out Melissa:

Melissa had lots of friends and she believed that she was living her best life. She traveled, purchased nice clothes and she had a nice home and car. She found herself out with friends every night. One night her friends decided that they wanted to add a little spice to their night life; hence, they went to a club that had a different spin to it. There was nudity, sex, smoking and lots of drinking and drugs. She noticed that most of her friends joined in and began to smoke. Melissa did not want to feel left out so she joined in as well. She even made a vow to herself that she would never smoke but what the heck, in her mind, she worked hard and deserved to have fun. Despite making a vow to herself to never smoke, her decision to smoke that night to smoke literally changed her life.

Melissa began visiting the club nightly and smoking on a regular basis. In 6 months her smoking habit went from occasional marijuana usage to regular cocaine usage. She began to experience major issues financially, mentally, physically and socially. She became paranoid and no longer trusted her friends. All the drugs she tried over the last 6 months changed the course of her life in the worst way. Melissa lost her job, her house and all of her friends because she was unable to stand her ground and set boundaries.

Well perhaps your experience is not drugs but we have all experienced situations where we claimed we would never do a particular thing. I said I would never date a married man but I did. Although, I was young and naïve we can all end up in situations that compromise who God created us to be. At the time I was dating the married man I did not understand how much God loved and valued me. I did not have my own values set in place. Therefore, I was unable to take a stand. My situation perhaps did not end as dramatically as Melissa's, but I did experience issues with my self-image when he rotated between me and his wife. He made promises to leave her and to start a life with me; nevertheless, it has been over twenty years and he is still with her. I remember vividly how that one decision changed my life.

Anytime we operate outside the areas that make up our core values and beliefs we begin to have value conflicts which could lead to stress, anxiety and other mental health challenges.

The Dump

1. Before making decisions, ask yourself, does the situation pose a value conflict for me? Does it line up with my strategies to live my best life?

2. How does this decision impact my relationship with God, my finances and my emotional well-being?

3. What will this decision cost me to correct? How much? What are the consequences?

Main Point: Know your values and align with people, places or things that support your values.

Pledge: I pledge to honor my values and set boundaries that support my values.

Reflection: Value conflicts will arise but you have the ability to reject areas that don't align with your values.

Chapter 7

Healing the Broke: Stop the Bleeding

Healing and forgiveness are crucial elements needed in establishing and maintaining boundaries. When you have unresolved issues that haunt you it becomes a challenge to set boundaries effectively. One of the primary reasons is due to lack of trust. In addition, hurt, disappointment, anger and frustration will blind you and force you to make decisions that are unhealthy or unstable.

See how brokenness affected Wanda's life

As Wanda reflected back over her life and wondered how she got to where she was today she was in shock. At one point, she had been described as cold, calculated and very much a skeptic. She had very rigid boundaries. For Wanda it had not always been that way. Wanda grew up in a very violent household. She experienced neglect, abuse and poor structure. So as she became an adult she became very rigid. Everything had to be a certain way, as she needed to maintain control in every aspect of life. As she began to date, she dated men that were never good enough for her. She also began to self-sabotage the relationships that appeared healthy and blamed the men in her life until she met David.

David was different; he penetrated the broken areas that Wanda experienced. He showed her love, he was patient with her and he treated her like a queen. She felt she could totally let her guard down and she did very quickly.

After the relationship progressed, David asked her to move to another state to be with him and Wanda was a little hesitant. Things felt too good to be true and she began to worry about the relationship despite how good David treated her. Eventually arguments began to ensue and she began to nit-pick at everything David did for her. David's personality changed and he started to talk to her in ways that made her feel uncomfortable. Wanda started to feel trapped, just as she did when she was a child. She felt like she was out of control. In turn, she started to take control by bossing David around. Her tone became very aggressive at times and she also started to become physical by throwing things around the house. David began staying away from the home and eventually asked her to leave. Wanda was devastated and began to question her life. The only option she could think of was suicide. So she attempted to take some pills and was hospitalized. Wanda could only think about things working out with her and David. She was obsessed with David to the point that she began to fixate herself on him which resulted in stalking.

The issue with Wanda is that she had not healed from her past wounds. Although David treated her well she was in a broken place and was unable to manage the emotions from this relationship. Without the necessary boundaries needed to heal she normally set rigid boundaries to protect her unmet needs.

Many of us have experienced the Wanda syndrome. Where we felt like we needed to set up the walls of Jericho for protection only to let the walls down and determine you are ill-equipped to manage the emotions that come with relationships.

Have you forgiven yourself and others for the harm caused? Often times we try to move fast through this step and have to back track. Forgiving the person who hurt you is not for them, it is for you. Forgiveness frees up space in your heart to love. Also forgiving yourself is one of the first step to forgiving someone else. If you are unable to offer grace to yourself it is less than likely you would be able to forgive others. Are you able to identify brokenness in yourself or others? If so, what does it look like?

Here are some of the tell-tell signs of brokenness: lack of trust or easily trusting, anger, sadness and several emotions can impact your ability to set a boundary. In addition, fear and irrational thoughts take over and you end up in a broken place.

When you are broken there is an excessive need to please. There are many more items we can add to this list but I share these areas because these are the top issues on my list of areas that kept me from setting appropriate boundaries for many years. It wasn't until I truly acknowledged my own brokenness that I could begin to heal and forgive. Through my pain, I found my purpose.

Growing up I had a wonderful childhood with two wonderful parents who gave me an amazing life. But God created a mother and a father for distinctly different reasons.

My mother was very protective and influential in my life; whereas, my father was the provider who appeared very focused on making sure we had a good life. Growing up the roles they played in my development appeared adequate; however, as I grew up I noticed that many of my choices and poor decisions in my relationships stemmed from me attempting to please and receive love. Mistake after mistake forced me to evaluate what I felt I was lacking. I so desired love and approval from a man. Ironically, I did receive love from my father; however, he showed love the way his mother taught him to show love, which was very different from what I needed. It wasn't until I realized that no love from a father, mother, boyfriend, or husband can substitute for God's love. I began to understand that God is the only one who can truly complete me. Sometimes I feel like I'm still healing from that pain, nonetheless I have forgiven my father and myself for the poor choices I knowingly made.

I know that God is my healer and my sustainer. You might be wondering what it means to be a sustainer. It means, God holds everything up in existence. He keeps things together;

he protects and continues to keep me. Before I knew it my pain pushed me towards healing which later pushed me towards my purpose. For some of you it will be a knock down drag out fight but do not give up.

The Dump

1. Have you acknowledged that you are broken and need healing and forgiveness?

2. Identify those who have harmed you and ask God to help you forgive them.

3. Have you asked God to forgive you? What scriptures highlight that you are forgiven.

4. Have a conversation with those that have harmed you and verbally let them know that you forgive them. For those who are deceased release yourself by writing a letter.

5. What actions have you taken to start the forgiveness process?

Main Point: Forgiveness is the first step in healing.

Pledge: I pledge to forgive myself and others.

Reflection: You must forgive to be forgiven.

Chapter 8

Stay In Your Lane:
What is Your Purpose?

I remember years ago reading a book called *Purpose Driven Life* by Rick Warren. The book highlighted ways to identify your purpose in God. It was a great read and millions of copies were sold but despite these numbers, I am sure there are millions of people who have yet to identify their purpose. At times, we are easily distracted by things going on around us. At times we can become easily distracted and we tend to think these areas are purposeful, but merely give us an illusion of purpose. When we do not incorporate rest into our daily lives it blocks us from clearly identifying our purpose.

Meet Stacey:

Stacey was very active in her church. She was a praise dancer, usher, and served on many ministries. Because she was extremely busy she was unable to understand the bible or what was taking place in church. She often felt like she was pulled in many conflicting directions. Stacey did not feel any peace and often times she felt overwhelmed. She knew that God had given her purpose but she was so busy, she could not hear Him clearly. How many of us stay so busy that we cannot hear from

God? Stacey eventually slowed down and began to hear God very clearly. God revealed to her that he wanted her to speak to teenage girls to encourage them and give them hope. She developed a ministry at her church doing just that, and it impacted many lives.

Setting boundaries and staying in your lane is very important. In a world where we are driven by pleasing others, making money, and staying busy it is important to seek authenticity and seek to do what you are passionate about. I spent over 15 years climbing the corporate ladder in Human Resources only to later find out that my God-given purpose was to serve God's people in a different way. What did this cost me? Time, finances, lives not being changed, and a depletion of resources.

The Dump

1. Pray and seek God about your purpose- Develop prayers that you can say daily regarding your purpose.

2. Identify 3 scriptures that you can use to stay on track regarding your purpose.

3. Identify your natural gifts.

4. Identify your spiritual gifts.

5. Identify those things or people that you need to remove from your life to help you live out your purpose.

Main Point: Seek out your purpose through prayer.

Pledge: I pledge to do things that align with my purpose.

Reflection: Operating in your gifts brings fulfillment and joy.

Chapter 9

Pancake and Waffles Please

Have you ever found yourself eating to reduce stress? It makes you feel good until your stomach starts to hurt. Oftentimes, to deaden the pain we use destructive measures to help us feel good. In my times of high stress I find myself eating excessively to provide comfort for my emotions. However the long-term effect on your body is not comforting.

Check out Tina's story:

Tina sat with her doctor in disgust and embarrassment as her doctor asked questions about her weight gain over the past year. She shared with her doctor that she had experienced grief due to a loss, several job changes, and a divorce. Tina shared that food was the only thing that provided her comfort and love. She said food made her feel good again about living. Many of us have our comfort food that makes us feel good about a situation.

I remember when my father was diagnosed with cancer, I ate to help myself cope with the things that changed rapidly with his health. The negative effects were vast and before I knew it I was 25 pounds heavier with high blood pressure and a high sugar count. All of those issues arose because I was unable to utilize impulse control and set limits regarding my eating and my health. With prayer, hard work, and a complete mindset, I was able to turn things around.

I work with numerous clients that struggle with emotional eating and I had to remind myself of those things that I've discovered with them. Our situations can improve if we're willing to put in the work to make them better. My advice in these situations is to seek God for strength; in addition, seek out professional help if you want healthier ways to cope with life's challenges.

The Dump

1. Identify stressful areas that could cause you to indulge in emotional eating. (This will help you establish where to set your boundaries)

2. Identify healthy things you can do besides eating when you have emotional discomfort. (Exercise impulse control)

3. Identify the negative consequences you have experienced from emotional eating. (These are reminders not to travel down the same path again.)

Main Point: Stress has a multitude of negative consequences.

Pledge: I pledge to find healthy ways to manage stress.

Reflection: Emotional eating will not reduce stress but it will cause other health problems.

Chapter 10

Friends How Many of Us Have Them

How many people have those friends who, when they call, you look at the phone and try to determine if you want to pick it up? It's not because you don't love them or you don't want to talk to them it's because sometimes talking to friends require work.

Do you know that relationships should be balanced? They should represent a give-and-take exchange. You should not feel completely drained when you get off the phone with your friends. One of that possibly happens is that individuals enter and develop friendships from a place of lack. We desire love from other people and sometimes we will do anything to get that love. Subsequently, when friends call and they want to 'dump', tell you everything that's going on in their life, or ask you for anything and everything, you become a dumpster for other's issues. You allow this because you receive a sense of affection, validation, or perhaps being needed. This begins a continuous cycle until you get frustrated or tired of being dumped on. This becomes upsetting not only for you but the other parties involved because you have allowed them to get comfortable with overstepping their boundaries.

As great as it may feel, you cannot get your needs met from another person and vice versa. I repeat, you cannot focus on getting your needs met from another person nor attempting to meet other's needs. Those empty places and those holes you have inside of you are those areas that can only be filled with the love of God. It is critical for you to be able to identify those broken places such as: grief, bad relationships, disappointments or financial instability that has left holes in your life.

One of the things you want to consider from the beginning as you start cultivating relationships is your unmet needs. There are moments we subconsciously make these unrealistic demands of others without realizing that we are doing so. We are entering relationships and friendships because there is a desire to be loved and connect. That desire is healthy; however, we put stipulations on others based on an unmet need within ourselves. Identify those holes that Christ can fill for you.

I know all too well about this area. Anyone who knows me knows that I am a friendly person and I do a great job at cultivating relationship. However, I have learned that not everyone has a purpose in your life. Everyone has a purpose in their life. Sometimes people need to be on the outside of your circle. It is my hope that those of us who love from the inside out, and are unable to set good parameters to manage our hearts, will find this chapter helpful.

I remember several years ago I met a young lady; we had a lot of things in common. We are from the same city and state, we had some of the same aspirations and goals, and we experienced similar relationship challenges among other things. We discovered that we had been through a lot of the same things and immediately we began bonding over the phone. Soon we were meeting up and hanging out. We moved very quickly in the beginning and started to really open ourselves up to each other. I learned a lot of things from this experience and my biggest take-away was, if you don't take time to cultivate your non-romantic relationships as you do your romantic relationships they will end in destruction. When you fail to get to know a person's heart you begin to make assumptions about the person and their character. The truth is, only God can reveal a person's character to you so you must be open to receive discernment from God.

Often times there are misunderstandings and judgment which leads to apologies, or the lack thereof, when we don't take the time properly nurture the relationships that we enter into. I distinctly remember this person began to accuse me and attack my character. She began to say things like, 'you are not a supportive person or you're not a good friend'. Essentially she was saying that I wasn't really meeting her needs so she began dumping the blame on me. I was really hurt by her comments because I couldn't understand how she could feel that way. Based on who I am as person, I felt that I was being a good friend and helpful resource for her. So I began to evaluate the true purpose of our connection.

What the Lord revealed to me is this: just as you nurture a new budding plant by fertilizing the soil so that the seed has a

76

healthy and strong foundation through daily monitoring of the temperature, food intake and water; henceforth, you must enact the same principle with your relationships.

God began to show me an illustration of how things grow and come into existence. If you take the sun away from a garden and pollute it with bad food, or allow people to trample on the soil it could rupture the foundation. Perhaps it was never a good foundation. The fertilization growth process in any relationship takes time and if you move to fast the plant will die. Thus, you put more water on it, give it more food or even bring it in the house, it will remain damaged. The same is relevant in our relationships, they too become unrepairable. We both had up our defenses and were unable to reconnect on the same level we were on initially. The good news is that we were not supposed to connect at that level in that season; it was not the purpose of our relationship at that time.

One of the things you should carefully do in every situation is pray about your connections and ask God why the person is in your life. If it's for a season or a short time be thankful for that person in your life for that timeframe. Don't try to turn everybody into your best friend in a day. God has placed several people in your life to hold that space for you and they will provide exactly what you need. They are going to provide exactly what you need.

I'm thankful that I have friends in my life that I can call on for prayer; my praying warriors. They are non-judgmental, and are able to go before God and speak to Him on my behalf. I have my fun friends. We can go out and have a good time and have face time. There are other people in my life that hold a different space.

In a nutshell, I'm suggesting that you pray about every relationship. Spend ample time with the person to determine where they fit. At times we can become very critical and dismiss people when we don't like something about them. Friends can hold varying spaces in your life; just make sure you cultivate the relationship. Be flexible but direct on your boundaries in friendships. Look at people with your eyes and your heart.

Listen to what people say and what they do. Actions and deeds are important.

So I'm sure you would like to know how my story ended. We were never able to reconcile that relationship. We may talk to each other once a year, randomly text or wish each other a happy birthday. I do pray for her, if she comes to mind, but there are no expectations on either part. The purpose of that relationship was for me to provide her resources to get her acclimated in her career. Since I wasn't secure in the relationships I already had and the people that God had centered around me already; I became greedy and wanted more. More came very quickly and more ended very quickly.

This scenario is not about this person and what she didn't do and what I didn't get, it was about me understanding how God has wired me. It's also about the people He has equipped and placed in my life to minster, love, support and hang out with me. He has filled every bucket and I don't need to place anyone else in that bucket unless I seek guidance from Him.

If you are not a believer in Christ and you don't understand the jargon of seeking God and understanding that aspect let me help you understand on a natural basis. When you enter into relationships you need to weigh out the cost. Determine if you have an unmet need, then you put boundaries in place to make sure you are right for the person and vice versa.

In the book *Developing Godly Relationships* the author illustrates stages for Godly relationships. I think it's an excellent idea to move through a relationship at a slower pace. Don't feel bad about keeping the relationship at a certain stage. Learn to set boundaries and say no if someone pushes the limits or say no to yourself if you are moving beyond where the relationship should go.

Setting boundaries will minimize frustration and confusion while developing friendships. We are looking for people to add to our lives. Evaluate yourself and make sure you are in a good place to enter a friendship. If God has given you an assignment to mentor and provide guidance, stay in your lane and just do that. Evaluate your relationships at different times to make sure you both have clear expectations for the friendship.

The Dump

1. Are you spending more time talking or listening on a phone call? Are your needs being met? Are you meeting the needs of others?

2. What relationships do you need to re-evaluate? How many relationships do you need to end?

3. What are some good foundational ingredients in healthy relationships?

4. What boundary challenges do you have in maintaining healthy relationships with others?

5. What unmet need do you have that you are looking for others to meet in your friendships?

Main Point: Evaluate the relationships in your life.

Pledge: I pledge to utilize God to get my needs met.

Reflection: Everyone is not meant to be my friend.

Chapter 11

Let's Talk About Sex Baby

When I was younger I did not have a concept of the purpose of sex. In my household it appeared that that sex was forbidden and that if you had sex you would get pregnant, have a baby and that your life would be ruined. Through my lens, sex appeared to be bad. I have very few memories about conversation in my household about the birds and the bees. Consequently, grade school did a good job of educating me quickly. Sex was considered cool and everyone was doing it. I learned that sex would get you a boyfriend and lots of cool material items. I was intrigued and wanted to know more about this trend everyone else was doing.

We all know what the bible says about sex, but what happens when you are raised in a household where you parents are not following Christ or the principles in the bible pertaining to sex. What if you are in a household where your parents are pastors and you feel convicted and condemned every time the subject about sex arises or what if you are in a household and learned that sex is a way to earn money to take care of your family? What happens when you get a confused child who desires to get what she is told that she cannot have and will use sex as a tool for self-pleasure?

God designed sex not to harm you but for your purposeful pleasure. He was careful to give us the limitations and boundaries regarding sex to protect us. Boundaries are important to God because sex was intended for procreation, intimacy and companionship with your mate. The boundaries set in place are not only to protect your heart but also to protect your mind and body from unwanted pregnancies and diseases.

The Word of God declares in 1 Thessalonians 4:3-5, "For this is the will of God, your sanctification that you abstain from sexual immorality; that each one of you know how to control his own body in holiness and honor, not in the passion of lust like the Gentiles." There is substantial evidence in the bible pertaining to uses of sex. It reflects that God's only intention for sex was under the confines and covenant of marriage. The sexual relationship is only properly expressed in marriage between a husband and wife, as specified in, 1Corthianians7:2-3.

Unfortunately, when sexual intimacy takes place out of the union of marriage there are numerous consequences that are costly and the effects at times are irreversible. In today's society sex is often used as a substitution for love. Sex has been used in several ways to include; to gain money, solicit drugs, and to implore human trafficking to name a few. Sex has caused severe trauma, left emotional scars and has become normalized in families who participate in sexual incest. It has also been used a form of manipulation and seduction at times for women to get their way.

My goal is not to portray sex as anything bad or horrid. It is not to scare people out of having sex, but to educate you on the implications of it when it is used outside of the purpose it was intended which can cause major destruction.

Listen to Melinda's story.

Melinda did not realize that when she woke up on this day that her life would change forever. A few days prior she remembered sitting in the doctor's office for a sprained ankle as she thought about the things she had to get done that day. She remembers the doctor taking her vitals and stating that her blood pressure was extremely high. The doctor did blood work and stated that he wanted to start her on some blood pressure medicine and sent her on her way. Two days later she received a call from the doctor who stated that they wanted her to come back in to run some additional blood test because her blood count seemed abnormal. After going to the doctor 2 to 3 more times the chilling news that she had HIV brought chills to her body. Melinda was devastated and perplexed. She felt fine, looked fine and instantly has to adapt to a new life. She begin to rack her brain about how could this happen. Melinda played back all of her sexual partners in her head. She thought to herself, I am a good woman, I only dealt with one guy at a time and for the most part she used condoms on a regular basis. The last relationship she was in she was engaged to be married so she had a rough time conceptualizing who she contracted the disease from. However, she felt it was her duty to reach out to those she came in contact with to notify them of her diagnosis. When Melinda called to speak with her ex fiancé about her diagnosis he was very quiet, she later found out that he had been diagnosed while they were engaged. He wasn't sure who he contracted it from, but he was in denial and hopeful he hadn't passed it along to her. He stated that he was very sorry that he did not warn her. He went on to say that's the reason why he broke it off with her. She was crushed, empty and unsure how she could go on and live her life. She desired so much to be married that she did not set the appropriate natural or spiritual boundaries to protect herself.

Although my story is different than Melinda's some of us all have traces of Melinda as it pertains to setting and adhering to appropriate boundaries regarding sex. I remember getting pregnant at 16 and having a miscarriage because I thought that love meant I needed to have sex. I remember the embarrassment of going to the doctor and him sharing with my parents that I had contracted a sexually transmitted disease (STD); I could barely pronounce the name of the STD. I recall looking at the doctor with a very innocent face wondering what is he talking about, I could barely even pronounce the words.

The disappointment my father had when he found out I was pregnant and the anger my mother had because she had warned me, caused me a lot of guilt and shame. Later, I found myself engaged to someone who was sexually abusive. I got pregnant by this person only to have an abortion because I did not want to have a baby by someone who forced me to have sex. I remember sleeping with a married man because the sex was really good only to realize later that God would not bless us and that I was destroying my body and also God's intention for marriage. One time, I even threw myself on a man only to be rejected, unwanted and unloved. I was haunted and depressed for years because of the abortions and miscarriages. There were countless times I used sex to meet my internal need for love. I always remember the void I feel when I think about having kids and the decision I made to destroy unborn children. I think of and feel the soul ties of the people I once had sex with and how difficult it is to get that person out of your mind. I could go on and on but I hope you get a visual of some of the consequences that can come from the improper use of sex.

I hope the person who is reading this chapter does not feel condemned but my hope is that you will be free to live in the present and not allow your mistakes of the past to haunt you and keep you in bondage. I am thankful for the cross and that I am forgiven by the blood of Jesus. The bible says in 1 John 1:9 that, "If we confess our sins, He is faithful and just and will forgive us for our sins and purify us from all unrighteousness." Confession is the first step to forgiveness.

I offer anyone reading this book the opportunity to accept Christ as your personal Lord, Savior, and friend. John 3:16 offers salvation to us all. He is the only one that has unconditional forgiveness. If you are not ready to accept Him as your Savior my suggestion is that you would seek counsel from a mental health professional that would help you begin the healing process.

The Dump

1. What sexual boundary violations do you need to admit, confess and ask God to forgive you of?

2. What needs were you attempting to get met by having sex?

3. What boundaries do you need to put in place to protect your body?

4. What emotional needs and consequences have come from sexual boundary violations?

Main Point: God designed sex and sexual boundaries to glorify Him and to protect you.

Pledge: I pledge to honor my body and to take care of God's creation by honoring His principles regarding sex.

Reflection: Your body is a beautiful creation and it should be protected.

Conclusion

Boundaries, boundaries and more boundaries. I hope you realize after reading my take on boundaries how prepared you already are for setting and maintaining life-changing boundaries. For those who feel like they need practice setting boundaries utilize the stories and the dump section given as a guide to monitor your choices and decisions to begin your process on setting boundaries.

God has given us all the ability to set boundaries and He requires this for our protection and self-preservation. He desires for us to live a life with restraints and limits, not to keep us from enjoying life, but to aid us in having the abundance of all that is good in life. We get to choose who we give our heart to, where we spend our finances, how much time we spend with our families, where we worship, what we listen to and how we live our lives. Begin to ask yourself are there areas of your life that you have neglected to set the proper limits? Are there any consequences or areas that you have been paying significantly in due to lack of boundary setting or awareness and insight in this area? No condemnation required. However, proper adjustments are necessary to allow you and I to live a life of purpose and fulfillment. Will setting boundaries make life perfect for you? The answer is affirmatively NO.

Nevertheless, effective boundary setting will help you learn to deal with life challenges more effectively because you will have a road map and a set of guidelines that tell you when to go, stop and proceed with caution. It is my sincere hope that after reading this book that you will exercise the power within to set, re-establish or maintain the needed boundaries for purposeful living. Just remember I am cheering for you as you go out and set powerful life-saving boundaries.

Are you on fertile ground or dumping Ground?

In the beginning of my book I gave you a visual of the "The Dumping Ground" Now I want to share a visual of fertile ground. Fertile ground is a safe place for growth. It's an area that is stable and protected by all of the good ingredients. When something toxic enters fertile ground it overtakes all the safety that the fertile ground provides. Setting life changing boundaries will allow you to have a fertile, mind, body and spirit.

3 ways to maintain a fertile ground:

- Allow the Holy Spirit to guide you

- Surround yourself with people who love you and will hold you accountable to take care of yourself. When you do not take care of yourself, you are telling God that you do not like or appreciate his finest creation.

- Reflect and ask God to give you the ability to set boundaries

HAPPY BOUNDARY SETTING!!!!!

Reviews

The chapter "Are You Willing to Pay the Price, really made me think about the impact of making decisions not aligned with my values and highest priorities. The examples from both the author and another person really amplified the need to set strong boundaries for a great life. Great read!
~Cledra Gross

The Dumping Ground touches on topics that are crucial to setting boundaries on time. Latasha does a good job of defining time and the importance of understanding what a precious commodity it is in order to create a life of balance and meaning. The exercises at the end are a great start to helping you identify where you've been de-valuing time in your life and how to begin the journey of respecting not only your time but the time of others.
~ Gwendolyn L. Young, GL Young Consulting

LaTasha pours her soul into this book. The chapter on sex is bold and captivating. The way that she engages you and requires you to take a long look in the mirror is riveting. This book is an absolute must read!"
~Tanisha Sapp

Buckle your seatbelt and hang on for a ride. With practical and relevant transparency, Latasha will show you how to dump the weight of life, set boundaries and succeed to new levels of discipline and freedom.
~ Vincent Campbell, Senior Pastor, The Faith Center

The Dumping Ground provides a lot of wisdom around friendships and how to set expectations and boundaries for these special kinds of relationships. The examples shared by the author are really powerful. They helped me to see that not all friendships are created equally and we must use sound judgment, and prayer, to determine the role people play in our lives and how intimate of a friendship we should cultivate with them. After reading this book I will definitely do an inventory of the people I have allowed into my inner circle to make sure that these relationships are healthy, positive, and mutually fulfilling.
~Venola Mason, Atlanta, GA

Chapter 7 focuses on lack of trust as an issue that holds us back. The example of Wanda struggling in relationship with David points to the truth that if we struggle with trust, we set ourselves up for failure by creating what we most fear. In Wanda's example, she learned distrust, poor boundaries, and rigidity to compensate for struggles in her childhood. Now, even though she is no longer a child, she clings to the child-like coping mechanisms despite no longer being in the dysfunctional environment. She meets David who treats her well, respects her, and loves her. Unconsciously, however, she is fearful that he can't be trusted so she begins to treat him as if he is not trustworthy. By doing that she is saying to David through her behavior, "I don't trust you and I expect our relationship to not work." So it's no surprise when the relationship falls apart. A very clear example of how Wanda created what she most feared.

As individuals, if we take the activities of the "Dumping Ground" seriously, we can rid ourselves of many of these self-defeating behaviors.

~W. David Lane, Ph.D., LPC, NCC, LMFT, AAMFT
Professor
Coordinator of Doctoral Education
Department of Counseling and Human Sciences
Penfield College of Mercer University

About the Author

Latasha Matthews, Owner/CEO of IllumiNation Counseling and Coaching, LLC and co-founder of Pieces that Fit, Inc. (501 3(C)) She has worked in higher education and corporate America. She has provided in-home community-based therapy, and worked in a variety of private practice settings. She is well-versed in providing individual, couples, family and play therapy techniques. With over seven years' experience as a marriage and family therapist, Latasha uses a Family Systems approach which considers how a particular system impacts an individual person or situation.

Latasha maintains a private practice working with a broad spectrum of clients in in Lawrenceville, GA. Versatile and multi-talented, articulate and inspiring; she is passionate about providing compassionate, collaborative therapy, insightful coaching, resourceful consulting, and empowering training. Her impactful services have the potential not only to change your experiences but also to change your entire life.

Latasha is very involved in her community and is single with no children.   She enjoys traveling, teaching, learning, tennis and now authorship.

For more information contact Latasha:

Website: www.thedumpinggroundbook.com
Email: info@thedumpingground.com

Dump Notes

Dump Notes

Dump Notes